THE MYSTERIOUS MARCH WIND

JESSICA P

A Magical St. Patrick's Day Adventure story for kids Aged 6-12.

THIS BOOK BELONGS

_____

_____

TABLE OF CONTENTS

THE LAST DAY OF WINTER	3
THE COLOR MYSTERY BEGINS	8
CLUES IN THE WIND	13
THE WINTER SPRITE'S TRAIL	18
SECRET OF THE SEASONS	23
RACE AGAINST TIME	28
THE SPRING SWITCH	34

The Last Day of Winter

Fiona O'Connell knew something was wrong the moment her wind chime stayed silent. It was the first day of March, and her special copper chime - the one Granny Siobhan had given her for luck - always sang on windy days. Always. But today, even though the trees outside her window were dancing like crazy, the chime hung perfectly still.

"That's weird," she whispered, pressing her nose against the cold glass. The wind was definitely there, whipping through the streets of Cloverbrook like it was late for a very important date. Yet something about it felt... different.

Downstairs, she heard her mom call out, "Fiona! You'll be late for the parade planning meeting!"

Right! The St. Patrick's Day parade! Fiona grabbed her green jacket - her favorite one with shamrock patches on the pockets - but stopped mid-motion.

Was it her imagination, or did the shamrocks look a bit... paler than usual?

Her jacket's shamrock patches looked paler than usual. Granny Siobhan had once told her shamrocks were lucky because they carried the balance of nature —earth, water, and sky in three perfect leaves. But right now, they looked... faded. Like the luck itself was vanishing.

She was still wondering about this when she met Marcus outside. Her best friend was already taking pictures with his lucky green camera, but he looked confused.

"Fiona!" Marcus waved his camera at her. "Something's wrong with my photos. Look!"

Fiona peered at the camera screen. Marcus had taken a picture of Mrs. Murphy's prize-winning garden - the one that won "Greenest Garden in Cloverbrook" three years in a row. But in the photo, the plants looked washed out, almost transparent in places.

"Maybe your camera's broken?" Fiona suggested, but Marcus shook his head. "I took ten pictures. They're all like this. And..." he lowered his voice, "look at the real garden."

Fiona turned to look at Mrs. Murphy's garden, and her mouth fell open. The plants weren't just pale in the photos - they were actually fading right before her eyes! The bright green leaves were turning see-through, like glass catching sunlight.

A strange wind gusted past them, and Fiona shivered. It wasn't a normal March wind - it was too... sparkly? Yes, there were definitely tiny sparkles in the air, like diamond dust or...

"Frost," Marcus said, snapping another picture. "But it's too warm for frost. Isn't it?"

Before Fiona could answer, they heard a sound like tinkling ice cubes. Both kids turned just in time to see something - or someone - zip around the corner of Pine Street. Whatever it was left a trail of swirling frost patterns on the sidewalk.

"Did you see that?" Fiona whispered excitedly.
Marcus nodded, his eyes wide. "Think it has something to do with the disappearing green?"

Another gust of the strange wind blew past, and this time, Fiona was sure she heard something - a laugh, maybe? Or crying? She couldn't tell which.

"Only one way to find out," she said, already starting to run. "Come on!"
But as they reached the corner, they found only empty street and more frost patterns - patterns that looked suspiciously like arrows pointing toward the old park at the edge of town.

Fiona pulled out her notebook - the one where she kept track of weird weather patterns. "First clue," she said, writing quickly. "Wind chime won't chime. Second clue: green things going transparent. Third clue: sparkly frost in March."

"Fourth clue," Marcus added, showing her his camera screen again. "These frost patterns are definitely not normal."

High above them, the March wind whirled and whispered, carrying away more colors with each passing moment.

And somewhere in Cloverbrook, someone - or something - was about to turn their town's St. Patrick's Day celebration into the strangest mystery they'd ever solved.

And there, running down the middle of Main Street, was a trail of fresh frost patterns leading straight to the park.

Marcus quickly photographed the patterns while Fiona compared them to the ones in the snowglobe. "They match!" she exclaimed. "And look - they make a kind of map!"

A cold gust of wind swirled around them, carrying what sounded like a child's laughter mixed with sobs. As they watched, the green street sign above them began to fade, turning transparent from the edges inward.

"We better solve this fast," Marcus said, checking his camera screen.

"According to my pictures, the green is disappearing faster than yesterday." Fiona clutched the snowglobe tightly. "Then we better get to the park before sunset. Something tells me our winter sprite might be there, and I have a feeling he's not just stealing green for fun."

As they headed toward the park, neither of them noticed Granny Siobhan watching from her shop window, a knowing smile on her face as she hung up a wind chime that sparkled with an unusual frost pattern of its own.

The Color Mystery Begins

The emergency town meeting was not going well. Fiona and Marcus sat in the back of the community center, watching as Mrs. Murphy waved her now completely transparent garden gloves in the air.

"First my roses turned see-through, then my shamrocks, and now even my gardening gloves!" she exclaimed. "How are we supposed to have a St. Patrick's Day parade if everything green keeps vanishing?"

The room erupted in worried chatter. Mr. O'Riley, who owned the costume shop, stood up next. "All my green leprechaun costumes are turning clear as glass. The parade is in two weeks - what are we going to do?"

Fiona felt a gentle tap on her shoulder. She turned to find Granny Siobhan standing there, her silver hair twinkling with what looked like tiny ice crystals.

"Interesting weather we're having, isn't it?" Granny's eyes sparkled mysteriously. She was wearing her garden shop apron, which was strangely untouched by the vanishing green phenomenon.

"Granny, your apron - it's still green! How come?" Fiona whispered.

Granny touched the fabric thoughtfully. "Oh, this old thing? It's protected by... let's just say, older magic than you'd think." She winked. "Some things are meant to last through all seasons, my dear."

"You know, there's an old Irish tale about a winter sprite who once tried to stop spring from coming. But that's just a silly story."

Marcus, who had been quietly taking pictures of the transparent objects people had brought to the meeting, suddenly perked up. "A winter sprite? Like Jack Frost?"

"Something like that," Granny smiled. "Though this one was quite young and had trouble controlling his powers. But as I said, just a story." She reached into her apron pocket and pulled out what looked like an ordinary snowglobe.

"Here, this might help with your investigation. "

10

Fiona took the snowglobe carefully. Inside was a tiny scene of their town park, but something was odd about it. "The trees in here are still green!"

"Are they now?" Granny said mysteriously. "You might want to compare them to the real park. Oh, and do be careful around sunset - that's when young winter sprites are most active." With another wink, she disappeared into the crowd.

Marcus leaned over to look at the snowglobe. "Your grandmother is kind of mysterious sometimes."

"Tell me about it," Fiona agreed. She held up the snowglobe to the light and gasped. Hidden in the swirling snow were tiny symbols that looked exactly like the frost patterns they'd seen earlier.

Suddenly, the strange wind returned, whistling through the cracks of the community center's windows. This time, it carried the faint sound of someone sniffling, as if crying.

"The park," both friends said at the same time.
They raced outside, but stopped short at the sight before them.
Every green traffic light in town had turned transparent. Cars were honking in confusion at each intersection.

Clues in the Wind

The park was nothing like Fiona and Marcus remembered. Every tree, bush, and blade of grass was turning transparent, like a garden made of glass. The wind whipped around them, colder than any March breeze should be.

Fiona pulled out Granny's snowglobe and held it up. "Look! The trees in here are still green, but they're in different spots than our park."

"Like it's showing us how things should be," Marcus said, snapping pictures of both the real park and the snowglobe. He stopped suddenly. "Fiona! The frost patterns - they're changing!"

He was right. The icy designs they'd been following were shifting, swirling into new shapes. In the fading afternoon light, they almost looked like words:

Too warm... Too bright... Help...

"Someone's trying to talk to us," Fiona whispered. She reached out to touch one of the frost patterns, but it melted instantly under her finger. A sad whisper echoed on the wind.

Just then, they heard the familiar tinkle of wind chimes. Granny Siobhan appeared on the path behind them, carrying a basket of what looked like completely normal, still-green plants.

"Granny!" Fiona called. "How are your plants still green when everything else is disappearing?"

Granny set down her basket with a mysterious smile. "Sometimes, dear, the oldest things are protected from the newest magic. But more importantly - have you figured out what the wind is trying to tell you?"

Marcus showed her the pictures on his camera. "The frost keeps making messages, but they melt too fast to read properly."

"Ah," Granny nodded. "If only there was a way to make frost last longer.

You know, when I was young, we used to make frost flowers in winter by mixing morning dew with moonlight..." She trailed off, looking meaningfully at the snowglobe in Fiona's hands.

Fiona gasped. "The snowglobe! It's full of permanent frost!"

"Is it now?" Granny's eyes twinkled. "How interesting. Oh, and you might want to visit the old wishing well at sunset. Some say that's when the veil between seasons is thinnest." With that cryptic comment, she picked up her basket and walked away, humming an Irish tune.

As if on cue, the sun began to set. The wind picked up, and suddenly all the transparent trees in the park started to sparkle. A figure darted between them - too fast to see clearly, but it left behind a trail of fresh frost.

"There!" Marcus pointed his camera, but the figure was gone. However, in his photo, they could see something the naked eye had missed - a small object dropping from the figure's hand.

They rushed to the spot and found a tiny silver key, covered in frost that didn't melt when they touched it.

:

"It must be important if the frost stays on it," Fiona said, comparing it to the patterns in the snowglobe. To their surprise, there was a miniature key in the globe's scene, right next to the wishing well.

The wind gusted again, stronger this time, and they heard what sounded like a child's voice carried on the breeze: "Find me... Please... Running out of time..."

Marcus checked his camera's screen one more time. "Fiona, look at this last picture. Is it just me, or does that blur look like... a boy made of ice?"

Before she could answer, every remaining green leaf in the park suddenly shimmered and turned transparent. The sun had almost set, and in the growing darkness, the frost patterns seemed to glow, creating a path that led straight to the old wishing well.

"Come on," Fiona said, clutching both the key and the snowglobe. "I think it's time we found out who's really behind this mystery."

As they headed toward the wishing well, neither of them noticed the temperature dropping rapidly, or the way their breath was starting to fog in the unusually cold March air. Winter, it seemed, wasn't ready to leave Cloverbrook just yet.

The Winter Sprite's Trail

The wishing well looked different at sunset. Shadows stretched long across Cloverbrook Park, and a strange, sparkling mist hung in the air. Fiona and Marcus approached carefully, their footsteps crunching on the ground that was becoming more frost than grass with each step.

"Something's not right," Marcus whispered, his camera clicking rapidly. "Look at how the frost is forming patterns."

The frost was indeed unusual. Instead of random crystals, it formed intricate designs that almost looked like a map - or a message. Each swirl and curve seemed deliberate, as if trying to tell a story.
At the bottom of the well, something moved.

A small figure huddled against the stone wall - no taller than Marcus's knee, made of what looked like living ice and swirling snow. His white-blue hair sparkled with tiny snowflakes, and when he looked up, his eyes were the color of a winter morning - pale blue with hints of silver.

"Jack Frost Jr.," Fiona breathed. She remembered Granny's stories about winter sprites, but she'd never imagined one would look so... young.
JJ wasn't what they expected. He wasn't laughing or causing mischief. He was crying.

"I didn't mean to," he whispered, his voice like wind through icy branches. "I just wanted to stay. Just a little longer."

Marcus lowered his camera. "Stay where? What are you talking about?"

The sprite's tears fell as tiny snowflakes, each one creating a perfect, intricate pattern on the well's stone floor.

"My father," he said. "He disappeared last winter. The seasonal magic is supposed to pass from parent to child, but without his pendant, I can't control my powers."

Fiona remembered the vanishing green, the transparent trees, the confused town. "So you're making everything winter because you're scared?"

JJ nodded. Each movement sent a cascade of frost patterns swirling around him. "If spring comes and I can't transition the seasons properly, I'll fade away. Just like my father."

Marcus's camera captured something extraordinary - the frost patterns around JJ were actually telling a story. Fragments of images showed a larger sprite (presumably his father) teaching a younger JJ about seasonal magic, then mysteriously disappearing.

"The pendant," JJ continued. "It's the key to controlling the seasonal transition. Without it, my magic goes wild. I'm trying to keep winter here because… because I'm afraid of what happens if I can't."

Fiona pulled out Granny's snowglobe. Remarkably, the tiny landscape inside seemed undisturbed by the sprite's emotional turmoil. "Your magic is hurting the town," she said gently. "People are losing their St. Patrick's Day parade. The green is disappearing."

JJ looked genuinely surprised. "I didn't mean to hurt anyone. I just… I just don't want to be alone."

The wind picked up, carrying the sound of a distant wind chime - one that sounded suspiciously like the one in Granny Siobhan's shop.

Marcus and Fiona exchanged a look. Their mystery was becoming something much more complicated than a simple case of missing color.
"We'll help you," Fiona said finally. "But you have to stop taking the green. Deal?"

JJ's tears stopped. The frost patterns around him shifted, forming what looked like a tentative smile.

Outside the well, the first stars of evening began to twinkle - some green, some silver, some caught between both colors.
The mystery of Cloverbrook was about to change forever.

23

Secret of the Seasons

The moment JJ mentioned his father's pendant, the entire wishing well transformed. Frost patterns danced across the stone walls, creating a living mural of seasonal magic that told a story far more complex than Fiona or Marcus could have imagined.

"The pendant isn't just a piece of jewelry," JJ explained, his icy form flickering with emotion. "It's the key to maintaining the balance between seasons. My father was the Guardian of Winter Transitions - a role passed down through generations of winter sprites."

Marcus's camera captured something extraordinary. Each frost pattern wasn't random - they were fragments of an intricate map showing invisible pathways between seasons.

Magical routes that connected winter to spring, hidden from human eyes but vital to the world's natural rhythm.

"When a seasonal guardian loses their pendant," JJ continued, his voice echoing like wind through hollow ice, "they lose their ability to guide the transition. Without it, the magic becomes unstable. That's why everything in Cloverbrook is turning transparent - I'm not controlling my powers."

Fiona noticed something peculiar in the snowglobe Granny had given her. The tiny landscape inside seemed to pulse with a hidden energy, and now she could see a miniature version of the pendant JJ described - a delicate silver thing etched with symbols that looked like intertwining snowflakes and budding leaves.

"Seasonal magic is about more than just changing weather," JJ said softly. "It's about maintaining the world's heartbeat. Each transition requires precise magical choreography. One missed step, and everything can fall out of balance."

The wind picked up, carrying with it the distant sound of a wind chime - the one from Granny Siobhan's shop. And then, as if summoned by the magical conversation, Granny herself stepped from the shadows.

Her garden apron was completely untouched by the surrounding frost, and in her hand, she held a pendant that looked exactly like the one JJ had described losing.

"Some guardians," Granny said, her eyes twinkling, "protect more than just seasons. Your father trusted me to keep this safe, JJ. And I trust you to restore the balance."

Marcus's camera clicked rapidly, capturing the moment. The pendant in Granny's hand wasn't just silver - it seemed to be made of something between metal and living light, with intricate etchings that seemed to move and change when you weren't looking directly at them.

JJ's entire form trembled. "That's... that's my father's pendant!"

But something in Granny's smile suggested this was far from a simple reunion. The secrets of seasonal magic were about to unfold, and Cloverbrook would never be the same.

Fiona realized they were standing at the center of something much bigger than a mysterious disappearing green. This was about the fundamental magic that kept the world turning, the delicate balance between winter's rest and spring's awakening.

"How did you get that?" JJ whispered, his icy form flickering between solid and transparent.

Granny simply winked. "Some guardians," she said, "protect more than just seasons."

The wind chimes continued their mysterious song, and around them, the world seemed to hold its breath - waiting.

Race Against Time

The pendant in Granny Siobhan's hand glowed with an otherworldly light, casting rainbow shadows through JJ's transparent form. But before anyone could reach for it, a tremendous gust of wind swept through Cloverbrook Park, nearly knocking Fiona and Marcus off their feet.

"The balance is shifting!" JJ cried out, his voice barely audible over the howling wind. "Without the proper transition magic, winter and spring are colliding!"

He was right. All around them, chaos erupted. Ice crystals formed on tree branches, only to melt and reform in seconds. The few remaining green things in town flickered like broken traffic lights between visible and transparent. In the distance, car alarms began wailing as their previously clear-as-glass green paint suddenly reappeared, then vanished again.

"Granny!" Fiona shouted over the wind. "Why didn't you tell us you had the pendant all along?"

But Granny Siobhan's usual mysterious smile had been replaced by a look of concern. "The pendant isn't ready," she explained. "It needs to recognize its new guardian. Your father," she turned to JJ, "brought this to me last winter when he realized he was fading. He knew you weren't prepared yet."
Marcus's camera worked overtime, capturing the wild scene around them. Through his lens, he spotted something nobody else had noticed. "Look!" he pointed to the screen. "The frost patterns are forming some kind of countdown!"

In the swirling snow and ice, magical symbols were appearing and disappearing, like a ticking clock made of frost. JJ's eyes widened with recognition. "The Spring Equinox deadline! If I don't master the transition magic by midnight tonight, winter will become permanent!"

As if to emphasize his point, another wave of magical energy pulsed through the town. At the community center, they could hear screams of surprise as the St. Patrick's Day parade decorations flickered in and out of existence.
"But how can JJ master years of guardian training in just a few hours?"

Fiona asked, clutching the snowglobe tightly. That's when she noticed something extraordinary - the miniature scene inside was changing, showing different patterns of seasonal transition.

"It's a training tool," Granny revealed. "Your father left it with me, JJ. Each scene demonstrates a different aspect of transition magic. But learning them all before midnight..."

"We'll help!" Marcus declared, already reviewing the magical patterns he'd photographed. "My camera's caught every frost pattern since this began. Maybe there's a pattern, something that can help JJ learn faster!"

JJ furrowed his brow, trying to summon the seasonal shift, but as he lifted his hands, the air around him crackled unpredictably. A sudden blast of icy wind sent frost spiraling in the wrong direction—onto Fiona's jacket instead of the nearest tree.

"Hey!" Fiona yelped, brushing off the ice.
JJ groaned. "It's not working. I can't control it."

Granny Siobhan chuckled. "Magic isn't about force, young one. Try again— this time, feel the balance instead of commanding it."

He took a deep breath, closing his eyes. Instead of pushing the winter away, he imagined guiding it, letting spring's warmth seep in naturally. This time, the frost melted from the trees in slow, shimmering waves, revealing tiny green buds beneath.

Fiona noticed her wind chime's ribbon floating on the breeze, pointing steadily toward the town square.

"The parade route," she gasped. "It's the perfect path for practicing the transition! All the decorations, the planned celebrations - it's like a ready-made magical ceremony!"

JJ's form solidified slightly with hope, but then another magical wave hit, stronger than before. Trees groaned as their branches shifted between winter bare and spring buds in seconds.

The temperature whiplashed between freezing and mild, sending clouds of steam rising from the ground.

"We have to hurry," Granny said, her voice urgent. "The pendant must be mastered through three trials - Understanding, Balance, and Acceptance. Each must be completed before midnight, or all of Cloverbrook will be trapped in an eternal winter."

The wind chimes sang louder, their melody somehow both hopeful and warning. Time was running out, and somewhere in the distance, the town clock began to strike eight.

Four hours until midnight.
Three trials to master.
Two seasons hanging in the balance.
One chance to get it right.

The Spring Switch

Midnight was approaching. The town square glowed with an ethereal mix of frost and flickering green light as JJ faced his final trial. The first two had been challenging enough - Understanding the delicate balance of seasonal magic through Granny's snowglobe lessons, and achieving Balance by practicing transitions along the parade route.

Now came Acceptance.

"Remember," Granny Siobhan said, holding out the pendant, "accepting change doesn't mean forgetting what was. Your father knew this."

JJ's transparent form shimmered in the moonlight. "But what if I'm not ready? What if I fail?"

"You won't," Fiona said firmly. She held up her wind chime, which had finally started singing again. "Listen - the wind believes in you too."

Marcus checked his camera one last time. "Look at all the patterns you've already mastered," he said, showing JJ the photos. "Each one more complex than the last. You're ready."

Around them, Cloverbrook held its breath. The St. Patrick's Day decorations hung suspended between visibility and transparency. Every tree, every blade of grass, every green thing waited for its fate to be decided.

JJ reached for the pendant with trembling hands of frost. The moment his fingers touched it, everything changed. The pendant burst into brilliant light, sending waves of magic rippling through the town. Ancient symbols of seasonal transition swirled through the air like dancing snowflakes.

"I remember now," JJ whispered, his eyes glowing with understanding. "Father didn't disappear - he became part of the seasonal magic itself. He's been teaching me all along, through the frost patterns, through the wind..."

As the town clock began to strike midnight, JJ raised the pendant high. His voice, once uncertain, rang out clear and strong:

"I, Jack Frost Junior, accept my role as Guardian of Winter Transitions. I welcome the change of seasons with an open heart."

The final chime struck.

A wave of transformation swept through Cloverbrook. Green burst back into existence everywhere - but not just any green. This was green touched by magic, sparkling with tiny frost patterns that made it more vibrant than ever. Trees sprouted leaves that shimmered with winter's farewell kiss. The parade decorations gleamed with an ethereal blend of seasonal magic.

JJ himself transformed. Though still clearly a winter sprite, his form stabilized into something new - a perfect balance of winter's frost and spring's promise. The pendant around his neck pulsed with the rhythm of changing seasons. "Thank you," he said to his friends, smiling through happy tears that fell as tiny snowflakes. "For helping me understand that endings aren't always endings. Sometimes they're just new beginnings in disguise."

Granny Siobhan nodded approvingly. "And now, Cloverbrook will have the most magical St. Patrick's Day parade in history - where winter's last snowflakes dance with spring's first flowers."

As if on cue, a gentle March wind swept through the town square, carrying the joyful sound of wind chimes. In its wake, it left something remarkable - a trail of shamrocks dusted with frost, each one a tiny reminder that magic exists in every transition, every ending, and every new beginning.

Fiona and Marcus exchanged triumphant grins. They had solved the mystery of the vanishing green, but they'd found something even better - a new friend who would make every change of season a magical adventure.

And high above Cloverbrook, the March wind sang its ancient song, celebrating the eternal dance of winter turning to spring, of endings becoming beginnings, and of friendship that could bridge any season.

THE END.

Made in the USA
Las Vegas, NV
11 March 2025